A KISS ON THE BOTTOM

First performed by the Sherman Theatre Company at the
Sherman Theatre, Cardiff, on 17th November 1991, with
the following cast:

Marlene	Menna Trussler
Lucy	Shelagh Gough
Grace	Joanna Field
Bev	Donna Edwards
June	Kathryn Dimery

Directed by Phil Clark
Designed by Nick MacLiammoir
Company Stage Management by Maggie Higgins

A Kiss on the Bottom

A comedy

Frank Vickery

Samuel French — London
New York - Toronto - Hollywood

ISBN 0 573 13004 3

Please see page iv for further copyright information

Printed at Redwood Books, Trowbridge, Wiltshire.

CAST

Marlene
Lucy
Grace
Bev
June

Nurse 1
Nurse 2
Domestic
Sister

Note: **Nurse 1** and **Nurse 2** are non-speaking roles and can
be played by assistant stage-managers. The actress
playing **June** can double as the **Domestic** and **Sister**.

SYNOPSIS OF SCENES

ACT I Scene 1 Thursday, late morning
Scene 2 The following Monday
Scene 3 Twenty-four hours later

ACT II Scene 1 The following Saturday afternoon
Scene 2 The following Thursday evening
Scene 3 The following Saturday

Time — the present

**Other plays by Frank Vickery published
by Samuel French Ltd:**

After I'm Gone (*One Act*)
All's Fair
Breaking the String
Erogenous Zones
Family Planning
Green Favours (*One Act*)
Loose Ends
A Night on the Tiles
A Night Out (*One Act*)
One O'Clock from the House
Spanish Lies
Split Ends (*One Act*)
Trivial Pursuits

For Menna,
whose inspiration, for me,
knows no bounds

And in celebration of
the life and works of Joanna Field

ACT I

Scene 1

A women's ward in East Glamorgan Hospital

There are three beds with chairs, etc., surrounding them, and each bed has a locker containing a water jug, tissues, personal belongings, "get well" cards and so on. The curtains are drawn around Grace's bed, DL. Marlene's bed is C. Marlene is nowhere to be seen—presumably, she is down gossiping in the solarium or the sluice. June's bed is DR. There is a colour television at the foot of this bed. June is fully dressed and is packing a few things into a weekend case. She is in her late twenties, with straight shoulder length hair, which she constantly places behind at least one ear. She is quietly spoken and reserved

Marlene enters, carrying a magazine. She wears a nightgown and slippers. She stands half in and half out of the doorway

Marlene (*calling to someone down the corridor*) Hallo Emrys, how are you? (*She doesn't wait for a reply*) Walking better today, I see. Be going home tomorrow, I s'pect. (*She moves into the ward and throws the magazine on to her bed*) Ahh, nice to see old Emrys up and about. Mind, I still say sixty-three is too old to be circumcised. (*She has a little laugh at the thought of it, then goes to June and stops her from packing her case*) All packed and ready to go, are you?

June smiles rather uncomfortably and nods

I wish to God I was going home.

June reaches for a bottle of squash on top of her locker

Oooh, are you taking that bottle of squash with you? 'Cos I'll have it if you're not going to bother. I do enjoy a drop of squash, I do see, but our Roy won't bring me some in, no matter how many times I ask.

June hands her the bottle

(*Surprised*) Ooh, thanks very much. (*She puts it on her locker*) Are you
sure? Anything else you got there? Books, magazines, I don't mind what.
Hey, your colour telly'd be nice.
June Oh ... no ... um. I'm afraid I ——
Marlene (*laughing*) I'm only joking you silly bugger. Still — we'll miss it
though, won't we? Well, me and Grace that is. (*She nods in Grace's
direction, still giggling*) Yes, it's back to watching *Murder She Wrote* in
the solarium for us. (*Calling*) What do you think, Grace? She's taken the
colour telly with her. (*She stands just behind June*) The woman in the bed
before you left her telly here for a good couple of days. Well *she* didn't
leave it here — her family did. We must have had a lend of it for the best
part of a week. It was until well after the funeral, I know that.

Pause

Like that she went. (*She snaps her fingers*) Course I'm telling you now
because you're going home, but I didn't say nothing before because you
looked the nervous type to me.

Pause. June puts fruit from her bedside into a carrier bag

Yes, just like that she went. (*She snaps her fingers again*) She was sharing
some of her grapes with me one minute, and the next — she was gone. I
don't touch 'em now. Grapes. I eat all fruit, mind. But I don't touch a grape —
not now.

June immediately hands Marlene the bag of fruit

Oooh, thanks very much. (*She puts the bag away in her locker*) Are you
sure? Hey, I hope you didn't think I was hinting or anything?
June No. No, of course not. They'll only go to waste.
Marlene Doing you a favour then, am I?

June nods and forces a smile

(*Sitting on a chair* R *of June's bed*) Packed everything away now, have
you? You haven't forgotten nothing? Soap? Flannel? What about your talc
I fancied with that lovely smell? Have you remembered to pack that?
June Yes.
Marlene (*disappointed*) There you are then.

June clips the case together

Shall I give you a hand? You're never going to manage that and the telly.

June Oh ... no. It's all right.

Marlene You don't want to strain yourself, mind.

June No. Really. They're not very heavy.

Marlene You want to be careful. You don't want to do too much too soon. I remember I was too weak to lift a spoon after I had *my* D and C.

June is highly embarrassed

Sure you can manage now?

June (*almost blurting it out*) Robert is picking me up.

Marlene Oooh. Robert? (*She gets up from the chair and sits on June's bed*) Who's he then?

June (*insisting*) A friend.

Marlene Oh ay, that's right. (*She pauses*) I see.

June (*trying to be assertive*) No you don't. You don't see anything. He's a very nice man with a very nice wife and they are both very kind to me and ... (*She becomes upset and stops. She searches her coat for a hanky but doesn't find one*)

Marlene Hang on a minute. (*She gets a box of tissues from her bed*)

June (*taking one and wiping her nose*) Thank you. I'm sorry.

Marlene (*looking into the box*) And I am — I've run out now. (*She holds up the empty box*) Only a joke. (*She takes the box and puts it in the plastic rubbish bag on the side of June's locker*) I'll have plenty later on. I've asked Roy to bring some in. (*She pauses*) What time is he coming then? This Robert?

June (*unzipping her case and looking for something*) Any time now.

Marlene He's the one who visited you last night, I suppose? (*She sits at the bottom of the bed*)

June (*annoyed*) Jenny was coming too. But something cropped up at the last minute.

Marlene (*nodding; not completely convinced*) Well, he must have got a good job, anyway.

June takes a deep breath — Marlene is clearly driving her crazy

Either that or he thinks a hell of a lot of you to take time off from work. (*She laughs*) I know this much, if I rang Roy at eleven o'clock in the morning to say I could come home, I'd be still stuck here till the end of his shift. And then perhaps he'd go home and have a bit of food first.

Pause

Doing well for himself, is he? This Robert?
June (*with difficulty*) He runs his own garage.
Marlene I knew it. I knew it. I said to Roy last night. I said, that man works
with his hands, I said. You can always tell, can't you? Well I can anyhow.
They've got that worn look about 'em, haven't they? And of course there's
always the dirt under the fingernails. No matter how hard they try, they
never seem to get it *all* out, can they? Can always see a little bit of black,
can't you? Mind you, I like it myself. Always a good sign of a man's man.
(*She pauses and quickly eyes June up*) I'm surprised *you* like a bit of rough,
though. I had you down for the more professional type. You know —
teacher ... accountant. Somebody in a suit.

*June moves to the R of Marlene's bed, empties the contents of her sponge bag
on it and throws them at Marlene. Marlene moves to the L and collects up the
things as they are thrown at her, delighted*

Oh lovely. Cotton wool balls?

June resignedly throws a plastic bag of cotton wool balls

I'll share them with Grace if you like.

*Bev enters with two nurses. They wheel on another bed, which contains
Lucy. Lucy is in her sixties. Her hair is pulled back very neatly from her
head. Bev moves June's bed table c. June moves c with her, taking her
suitcase and the television. Nurse 1 collects June's locker and passes it to
Nurse 2, who takes it off stage. Nurse 1 and Bev move June's bed out of the
way,* DR

Bev Gangway, girls. Sorry, June, my love, but I've got to chuck you out.
You're just about ready anyway by the look of it. One in, one out.

Bev and Nurse 1 wheel Lucy's bed into position

Nurse 1 exits

It's all go in this place. (*To Lucy*) I'll be back with you now, my love. (*To
June*) Come on then, June. Let's get you on the road.
June I'm waiting for my lift. I'm sure he won't ——

Bev He's here. He's waiting for you down in the day room. Come on ... let me give you a hand with that.

She picks up the television and exits

Marlene (*moving towards June*) It's none of my business, of course ——
June (*sharply*) No. (*Less sharp*) You're right. (*She pauses; she means "it is none of your business"*) You're absolutely right.
Marlene Believe me, love, no good'll come of it. I know.

June just stares at her

Not that I've ever had a fling, mind. Not since I've been with our Roy — had plenty before — but not since. One dog one bone, that's me now, love. (*She pauses*) See, it's bad enough under normal circumstances but when you're friends with the wife as well ... you're too nice and too soft, I s'pect, which is probably how it all started in the first place.

Pause

Well, am I right?

June stares into space

If you were the sort that didn't give a damn you might stand a chance — but you're not see, love, are you? Either way, in my book you're going to end up ——
June Say goodbye for me to the lady at the end.

June exits

Pause. Marlene has a good look at Lucy

Marlene (*referring to June*) Lovely girl. (*She starts putting away all the things on her bed*)

Lucy watches her

She insisted on giving me these few things, see. I told her I didn't have any use for them. Anyway — (*introducing herself*) Marlene. Marlene Morgan.
Lucy Lucy Collier.

Grace (*callling from behind her curtained bed*) Excuse me, but I need a
nurse.

*Grace is seventyish. A little grand. She had money once but it has all gone
now*

Marlene (*crossing to Grace's bed*) Finished, have you, Grace?
Grace I would like someone to come and see me.
Marlene Beverley will be here now. She's got to come back to get rid of this
other bed.
Grace I don't want her, I want someone else!
Marlene (*to Lucy, as she crosses back to her bed*) She don't like her for some
reason. I don't know why 'cos she's marvellous with her. My own daughter
wouldn't do for me what she's done for her. You got children?
Lucy Only one.
Marlene Two, I got. The girl is mine by Roy — that's my husband — but
the boy is a love child. I was only seventeen.
Lucy Raymond will be forty this year.
Marlene (*referring to Grace*) She haven't got any kids. She pretends to like
'em but she hates 'em really. My sister's kids can't stand her. She called
them over to her when they came to visit me on a Sunday and they didn't
want to go. They're frightened of her. She doesn't look well, mind.
(*Quietly*) She's gone — she looks awful and I haven't got the heart to tell
her, see. And it wouldn't be so bad if she didn't ask me. But that's all she
does. She'll ask you too, I s'pect. She's asks everybody. Obsessed with
how she looks, she is. You get fed up with her after a bit 'cos that's all you'll
get out of her. "How do I look?" ... "Do I look all right?" You feel you don't
know what to say to her in the end. (*She moves to* R *of her own bed*)
Lucy Have you been in long?
Marlene Just over a week.
Lucy It's nearly a month for me. I've had my stitches out over a fortnight ago.
Marlene Why are they keeping you in then? What was the matter?
Lucy (*with relish*) I couldn't keep anything down. I'd have something to eat
and ten minutes later I'd have it all back.
Marlene I'm like that, see — only not all the time. Some days I can eat like
a horse. Others I can't even look at an egg without having it back. Did they
say what was wrong?
Lucy Some sort of blockage.
Marlene They haven't told me nothing yet. I'm still having tests. (*She
crosses to Lucy's bed*) Between me and you I've had just about a gut's full
here, though. They take so long to tell you anything. And they don't care
what they put you through. Do you know, there isn't a part of me that

haven't had something or other shoved up inside it. Oh I'm not complaining, mind. In fact, some of it was quite pleasant — (*she winks*) if you know what I mean. I wouldn't show them that though. Mind you, I had to go and have one of them barium enemas last Tuesday. I didn't enjoy that. Have you ever had one of those?

Lucy I've had everything. I've been back and fro here for eighteen months.

Marlene Almost a resident then? They told me yesterday I might have to have a bag. No, I said, not unless I can have a pair of shoes to match. (*She laughs at her own joke*) Oh you've got to laugh, haven't you? (*She pauses*) Grace have been in a long time. (*Raising her voice*) Haven't you, Grace?

Grace I beg your pardon, dear?

Marlene (*crossing* DR *of Grace's bed*) I said you've been in here a long time.

Grace Yes. Is someone getting me a nurse?

Marlene We've had a new one in, Grace.

Grace Ask her to come and tend to me then, will you, dear? I really do want to get back into bed.

Marlene I mean a patient. Little June have left. We've got ... what's your name again?

Lucy Lucy.

Marlene We've got Lucy in her place.

Grace Is she SRN?

Marlene She's not a nurse. (*To Lucy, as she moves* C) She always gets the wrong end of the stick.

Grace (*insisting*) SRN. I don't want to be seen by anyone less qualified.

Marlene You only want someone to wipe your arse. (*She pauses*) Shall *I* come and do it for you?

Grace Certainly not! I prefer a member of staff.

Marlene What's the matter? Don't you trust me or something?

Grace I'd rather wait!

Marlene (*not really offended*) Please your bloody self then. (*To Lucy*) I've offered. Can't do anything else, can I? (*She moves towards Lucy's bed*) I've always fancied myself as a bit of a nurse. I've got the stomach for it, see. Takes a special kind of person somehow — doesn't it? And I've never minded a bit of ... shall I prop you up a bit? You're sinking by the minute by there. (*She pulls Lucy into a sitting position, very roughly*)

Lucy Thank you. I was going to ask someone when they come to take the bed.

Pause

I haven't asked about going home. I'm not in any hurry.

Marlene I can't wait to go home, I can't. I had a sound scan yesterday and once they've had the result of that I'm hoping they're going to let me go. Live on your own, do you?

Lucy I buried my husband. Raymond comes down as often as he can but it's not easy to get away. Not with his job. And of course there's Hazel, that's his wife. She's very good to me. I rarely see her but she's very good to me. She seldom misses sending a birthday or Christmas card. Raymond has invited me up — they live in Surrey — but it's not a big house, they say, and I wouldn't like to put the girls out. I've got two granddaughters. Eighteen and twenty-one. Need a lot of space at that age, don't they? I've got photos. I'll show you when they bring my things. (*She pauses*) I wish they'd write to me though. (*She smiles*) Boys. That's all they're into now.

Marlene Well I can't say nothing about that. I was exactly the same at their age. *And* you were too, I s'pect.

Lucy Only one man I ever had and we didn't meet until I was well into my twenties.

Marlene Never. Good God, I had twenty before I left school. It wasn't as if I was fast or loose or anything like that. It's just that I hated girls. They bored me to death. I couldn't stand all that girl talk and giggling. I'd rather flirt with a boy any day.

Bev enters with Lucy's locker. She sets it in position

Bev Sorry I've been so long, girls.

Marlene Oooh hey, Bev — Grace is waiting for you. She needs a hand — literally.

Bev (*raising her voice a little*) Won't be a minute, Grace. Just going to get rid of the bed.

She goes to the empty bed, pushes it off and enters

Marlene (*to Bev*) She has been waiting for a long time. (*She moves to the foot of Lucy's bed*)

Bev We're short this morning, Ma. We're two down.

Marlene Haven't had the chance to see if my results are back then?

Bev Marlene, I've been dying for a pee for the past hour and a half. I'm hoping to put one in now about eleven o'clock.

Marlene Point taken. But you will let me know as soon as they're here, won't you?

Bev They *are* here.

Marlene What?

Bev Doctor Fairwater is going to come and have a word with you this afternoon.

Marlene Oh, I can't wait that long. You can have a peek for me can't you, and tell me if everything's all right?

Bev doesn't answer. She turns to leave the ward

Bev (*calling to Grace*) Be back in a minute, Grace.

Bev exits

Pause; Marlene stands motionless

Marlene Why did they take so long? All my other results came back the following day. (*She crosses to the side of Lucy's bed,* L) Are you under him as well? Fairwater?

Lucy nods

I've *got* to be home for next week. My daughter's getting married a week on Saturday. Lucky, I saw to most of the arrangements before I came in. I'd have said no otherwise.
Lucy To what?
Marlene (*moving to the foot of Lucy's bed*) Coming in for tests. I said to Roy, I said, "Trust 'em to send for me now", I said. I've been waiting for 'em to get in touch for weeks. "Go in and get it sorted, with a bit of luck you'll be out for the big day", he said. (*She tries to laugh*) I miss this wedding and I'll bloody crown him. (*She laughs again but she is very worried*)
Lucy Does he know about the wedding? The doctor, I mean?
Marlene They *all* know. I made sure I told every bugger the day I came in.
Lucy I'm sure they'll do what they can.
Marlene I paid a fortune for my outfit. (*She moves back to the* L *side of her own bed*) It fitted perfect when I bought it. I'll have to have it taken in a bit now — I've lost a bit of weight lately.

Bev enters and heads straight for Grace's bed

(*Stopping her before she disappears behind the curtains*) You've already seen 'em, haven't you?

Pause

Bev Doctor will explain it better than me.

Marlene I'd rather hear it from you.
Bev It's nothing to worry about at this stage.
Marlene What's it all about then?
Bev He wants to do more tests.
Marlene (*relieved*) Oh is that all. You had me going ... you frightened me
a bit by there then.
Bev Well, it's more of an investigation really.
Marlene You mean they want to open me up?
Bev It's the only way of being absolutely sure, Marlene.
Marlene Of what?

Pause

Bev Well, like I said ... the doctor can explain it better than me.
Marlene So it's not an operation then?
Bev Oh yes. Well, you'll have anaesthetic and that. They'll do tests on the
operating table and they might decide to operate, depending on what they
find.

Pause

Marlene I see. (*She pauses*) When am I having it done?

Pause

Bev Monday.

Pause

Grace (*calling from behind the curtains*) Nurse!
Bev All right, Grace ... it's your turn. You've got a choice this morning.
Which hand do you want ... my right or my left? (*She disappears behind
the curtains*)

*Marlene gets into her bed and sits up straight. She looks over to Lucy, then
looks out front, a worried expression on her face*

Black-out. Music:"District Nurse"

Scene 2

The same

The following Monday, about eleven a.m.

The Lights come up and Marlene is discovered lying on her bed, now wearing a theatre gown and a surgical paper hat

Bev draws back the curtains around Grace's bed and exits

Grace sits upright, putting on make-up. She wears a wig. Lucy is also sitting upright, reading a letter from her son. A photograph of him and his family is now proudly displayed on her bedside cabinet

Lucy (*excited*) They're coming down. They all are — Raymond, Hazel *and* the girls. (*She continues reading her letter*)
Grace (*referring to her compact*) There used to be a mirror in this.
Lucy When is the twenty-third?
Grace Why has someone taken the mirror out of my compact?
Marlene It's the sixteenth on Saturday.
Lucy They can't make it before because of the car ... it needs servicing and the garage can't fit it in for a week.
Marlene That sounds like a load of old bull to me.
Lucy No, he's very careful with things like that. He won't drive it a mile over what it's supposed to.
Marlene What's the matter with the train then? The car needing a service wouldn't stop me from seeing *my* mother.
Lucy It would cost a lost of money for them all to come by rail. And if it means I'm going to see the girls, I don't mind waiting an extra week.
Marlene You are soft in the head, you are — you know that, don't you?
Grace I can't see what I'm doing. Sit up and have a look, will you?

Pause

Marlene You talking to me, Grace?
Grace I want to know how I look.
Marlene Tell her how she looks, Luce.
Lucy You look lovely.
Grace I want the other woman to see.
Marlene I've had my pre-med, Grace. I don't know if I can lift my head.
Grace Well try, there's a dear.

Marlene (*sitting upright without any effort*) I shouldn't feel like this.
Lucy What's the matter?
Marlene I don't feel any different. I don't think it have taken. I've been waiting here so long I bet the bloody thing have worn off.
Lucy Come to think of it, you have been waiting a long time.
Grace (*to Marlene*) Well? Tell me the truth. How am I looking?
Marlene (*looking towards Grace; saying it even though Grace looks pretty dreadful*) Beautiful. You're looking beautiful. A lot better today, honest (*She gets off her bed*)
Lucy I don't think you should get off the bed.
Marlene I'm only going to comb her hair.

Marlene crosses to L side of Grace's bed and takes the powder compact. During the following, she rubs some powder from Grace's face and puts a little rouge on her cheeks, and maybe some lipstick on her lips. Then she makes a little adjustment to Grace's hair

Lucy I think I might be going home.
Marlene Why?
Lucy Raymond's coming for a reason. Perhaps they're going to air the house or something.
Grace (*to Marlene*) What's the matter with the one on the end?
Marlene Lucy?

Grace nods

She's had an operation.
Grace (*impatiently*) Yes yes, I understand that, but why? What has she had done?
Marlene She had a blockage.
Grace Where?
Marlene I'm not sure. The bowel, I think.
Grace Large or small?
Marlene I don't know.
Grace Has she had everything taken away?
Marlene I'll have 'em come and take you away, you keep on.
Grace They say that's what they've done to me. I'll soon be on the mend, they said, but I still feel as ill as ever. (*She pauses*) Gilbert tells me I'm coming on in leaps and bounds — but I feel just as ill as before — worse even. Are you sure I look all right?
Lucy (*still reading her letter*) That's funny.

Marlene looks over to her

They're coming on a Friday. They've never done that before.
Marlene Think there's something up, do you?
Lucy I don't know.
Marlene Are they on the phone?
Lucy Yes, but I haven't got their number.
Marlene (*amazed*) What?
Lucy Raymond rings me once a week. He says he doesn't want me to run my bill up by ringing him ... and Hazel said that the number is too long for me to cope with. It *is* on the long side, what with the area code as well.
Marlene So you can't give them a call then?

Pause

Lucy Not really.
Marlene Do you know their address?
Lucy I have it written down. (*She looks for it in her handbag*)
Grace (*to Marlene*) Is Gilbert coming today?
Marlene Gilbert comes every day.
Grace Then why isn't he here?
Marlene Because it's only quarter past eleven and he doesn't come until the afternoon. (*Finishing with the make-up*) How's that?
Grace I wish I had a mirror. You wouldn't have one I suppose?
Marlene Yes love, I got one. (*She goes to her bed to get her make-up bag*)
Lucy (*noticing Marlene*) Er ... no. (*To Marlene; confidentially*) I wouldn't. They try not to.
Marlene (*softly*) What?
Lucy It's best she doesn't. It's an awful shock sometimes.
Marlene (*nodding, realizing the situation*) Er ... sorry Grace—I don't know where I've put it, love.
Grace Not to worry. They've probably taken yours too.

This hadn't occurred to Marlene. Panicked, knowing what it might mean if it has been taken, she desperately looks for it in the bag. She finds it, much to her relief. She puts the bag back in her locker

Marlene If they don't hurry up I'm going to have something to eat.
Lucy You can't do that.
Marlene I haven't ate bugger all since eight o'clock last night. I'm starving.
Lucy You mustn't — not with the anaesthetic. You won't be able to have your investigation.

Marlene I don't care anymore. It's not fair to keep me waiting all this time.
Grace (*very grand*) Gilbert never keeps *me* waiting.
Marlene I bet he'd never dare.
Grace Always on time. I like that.
Marlene (*moving to the* L *of Lucy's bed*) If I kept Roy waiting when we were
    courting — and I did more than once — he wouldn't hang about. I always
    knew where to find him though. I'd only have to look for the nearest pub.

Bev enters, sporting a beautiful black eye

Bev Marlene! What are you doing on your feet?
Marlene I got fed up laying on my back.
Bev I heard that was your favourite position.
Marlene Who told you that?
Bev Treorchy Rugby Club. Come on — on the bed please.

Marlene jumps on to her bed and Bev pulls a blanket over her

Marlene Is this it, then? Have you come to fetch me?
Bev No. We've had an emergency. I'll find out exactly what's happening
    now, but I think we might be cancelling you until tomorrow.
Marlene No — you can't do that.
Bev It's out of my hands, love.
Marlene If I don't have it done today that means I'll have to have it
    tomorrow.
Bev That's right.
Marlene But that'll bugger things up good and proper.
Grace Nurse?
Bev Yes, Grace?

Marlene pouts as she takes in the full consequence of the possible delay

Grace How do I look?
Bev (*moving to Grace*) What have you done to yourself?
Grace That common woman came and combed my hair.

Bev moves around Grace's bed, tidying it as she goes

    She reminds me of someone. How long before Gilbert arrives? (*Remem-
    bering*) I know — I had a charlady like her.
Bev Two o'clock is about his time. You've got a couple of hours yet.
    Everything else all right otherwise?

Grace I have a constant feeling of nausea.
Bev Do you want me to get you something?
Grace Would you?
Bev (*about to leave*) I'll be back in a tick.
Grace You're not getting me a receiver, are you?
Bev I'm getting you an injection.
Grace Oh dear ... not another prick.
Bev That you should be so lucky, love.
Lucy (*calling to Bev*) Nurse, have you heard if I'm being discharged?
Bev (*crossing to her*) No, not a dickie bird.
Lucy My son is coming down from Surrey. (*She gives Bev the letter*) I
thought perhaps he was taking me home.

*Bev hands it back with a sad smile and a slight shake of the head. A slight
pause*

Bev What about you, Marlene? Can I get anything for *you*?
Marlene (*sitting up*) I'd either like a trolley to take me to theatre, or I'll have
pie and chips.
Bev I reckon that's half your trouble — too much greasy food.
Marlene The trolley then. (*She lies down and takes her hat off*)
Bev (*turning as she goes*) I won't be long, Grace.

She exits

Marlene I'm going to scream if I don't end up having it done today.

Lucy looks at her

They know how important it is for me to have it now. (*She sits up*) Saturday
will be here before we know it.

Pause

Lucy No-one have said anything about the nurse's eye.
Marlene She'll have another bugger to go with it if I don't get down that
theatre today.
Lucy It's not her fault.
Marlene (*sighing*) No, I know.
Lucy I wonder how she had it.
Marlene Ask her. I'm sure she'll tell you.
Lucy Oh no — I wouldn't have the nerve.

Marlene It's looking awful sore with her. She should have had a day off.

Lucy She didn't work over the weekend. She probably hasn't got another day coming.

Marlene She could have a day sick.

Lucy Good thing she didn't. They're short-staffed already. Didn't you hear her say?

Marlene This hospital will be here after her. There's nothing wrong in having a day for the queen. She do work hard, that kid do. Apart from her eye she's been looking shattered lately. I wouldn't mind betting she spent the weekend in bed.

Lucy No — she was going away. She did say, but I can't remember where.

Marlene She's got a caravan in Mumbles.

Lucy That's it — Mumbles.

Marlene I wonder if she lets it out? Perhaps she'll let it to me. I wouldn't mind a little week away — help me over this little lot, if I ever have it.

Lucy When Raymond was small, we used to have a caravan every year in Porthcawl. It was never a holiday for *me* though. It wasn't for any woman. Still isn't as far as I know.

Marlene Ooooh, I've told our Roy — I'm not washing a bloody dish when I get out of here. He's going to have to do the lot for at least a month. It's not so bad for him *now* 'cos our Louise is there — but she'll have her own house to take care of after Saturday.

Grace It's a shame you having to miss her wedding.

Lucy She's still keeping her fingers crossed.

Marlene It's only Monday *now*, Grace. If I end up having it done today and everything turns out all right, I should be out by Wednesday at the latest.

Grace I wouldn't put your mind on it.

Marlene I'll get to see her on the day either way, she said. If I end up having some sort of op and I got to stay in, she said she's coming here first with her father, and then coming back after the reception with Wayne.

Pause

Grace My mother never came to *my* wedding. She didn't approve of Gilbert.

Marlene Roy threatened not to come to ours. If it wasn't that my father owned an airgun, I don't think he'd have bothered.

Grace Your husband doesn't approve of firearms?

Marlene Not when they're sticking into the back of your neck — no. I'm the *best* thing that's happened to Roy though. And he'll tell you that himself — when he's drunk. God knows how he'd have turned out if it wasn't for me. Alcoholic, I shouldn't wonder.

Grace She grew to like him eventually of course.

Marlene and Lucy turn to look at her

Gilbert. (*She pauses*) My mother. He nursed her right up until she ...

Pause

Marlene Roy's been good to me too, mind. And he's always worked — I'll say that for him. He's never had a lot of brains, but there's nothing wrong with a bit of brawn now and again. What do *you* say, Luce?

Lucy coyly covers a smile

And he's never once laid a finger on me. I'll put up with a lot but I won't stand for that. It wouldn't pay him to give me a clout, anyway — I'm bigger than he is. Or I was — I've lost a bit of weight lately.

Slight pause

Grace Gilbert and I used to knock each other about rather a lot. It was our form of foreplay.
Marlene Roy's idea of foreplay is half a dozen pints of lager and a game of darts.

Bev enters

Bev (*going to Marlene's bed*) Guess what, Marlene? It's on.
Marlene What is?
Bev I've got a porter outside waiting to take you down.
Lucy (*to Marlene*) There you are — everything's falling into place. I'll keep my fingers crossed for you.
Marlene Ay — and everything else.
Bev (*to Marlene*) Are you ready? Shall I send him in?
Marlene Let me put my hat on first. (*She does*)
Bev Very nice, too
Marlene Bugger off.
Bev Fit?
Marlene If I was fit I wouldn't be done up like this.
Bev Now, you're not worried or anything now, are you?
Marlene Worried? I'm bloody shitting myself.
Bev Want me to come down with you?

Marlene (*shaking her head*) No need for that.

Bev Two hours and you'll be back in bed.

Marlene What time do you knock off?

Bev Oh, I'll come and see you and make sure you're all right before I go home, don't you worry.

Marlene Come on then ... let's get this show on the road.

Bev (*opening the door and calling to the porter*) She's ready when you are Mr DeMille.

Black-out. Music: "Doctor Kildare"

Scene 3

Twenty-four hours later

The Lights come up. Marlene is sitting in an armchair. She is attached to a drip — her investigation turned into a more serious operation. She is a little weaker than she was, but still as sharp as ever. Grace is also sitting in an armchair, reading a magazine. Lucy's bed is empty and unmade— she is out of the ward at present. After a second or two Bev pops in. Her eye is not as bad as it was

Bev It's very quiet in here. How's my favourite girls do in 't?

Marlene Favourites? I bet you say that to every bugger.

Bev No I don't.

Marlene I've heard you in the other wards.

Bev Yeah but I mean it with you two. (*She checks the drip*)

Marlene How long have I got to be attached to this thing?

Bev If this stand had a mouth, Marlene, it would probably ask me the same thing. (*She has a little laugh*) Only a day or two — that's all I expect.

Marlene I want to get back into bed, Bev.

Bev (*checking her watch*) Try and stick it for another ten minutes.

Marlene I couldn't believe it when they got me out of bed this morning.

Bev Aaahh, we don't hang about these days.

Marlene That's a nasty black eye you've got.

Bev It's going now — thank God.

Marlene Lucy was wondering how you got it.

Bev And you weren't?

Marlene It had crossed my mind.

Bev I fell down stairs.

Marlene Ay — and I got wings sprouting out of my back.

Bev (*insisting*) I did. (*She tidies up around Marlene's bed*)

Marlene If I believe that, I'll believe anything. And anyway, caravans don't have stairs.

Bev (*smiling*) How do you know I've got a caravan?

Marlene Never mind how I know — tell me what happened to your eye.

Bev My stair carpet was a bit loose. Luckily I fell *up* the stairs and not down, or I would have had more bruising than this.

Marlene Hang about a minute by here now. *You* just said you fell *down* the stairs.

Bev No I didn't.

Marlene Yes you did.

Bev Well I meant up.

Marlene I can't swallow that, somehow.

Bev You can't swallow anything at the moment, Marlene — that's why you're on a drip, love. (*She has another little laugh*)

Marlene You know exactly what I meant.

Pause

Somebody have been giving you a clout, haven't they?

Bev It's nothing I can't handle.

Marlene You're a lovely girl and I don't like the thought of you being knocked about. If anyone's giving you trouble let me know. Our Darren used to be in the TAs.

Bev Ooohhh, a soldier — give me his name and address.

Marlene Handsome boy. Big lump of a thing. He's seventeen and a half collar. He's into all this "body beautiful".

Bev Oh, I'm going before I come over all funny. (*She makes to leave*)

Marlene No, don't go — stay here a minute.

Bev sits on Marlene's bed

Look, I know I got a bit of a chops on me, right? But me an you get on OK, don't we? What I mean is — if you need somebody — just to listen like — I wouldn't interfere — you know where I am. Got me?

Bev (*smiling and nodding*) Got you.

Pause; Bev starts to leave, then stops by Grace

You all right, Grace?

Grace I'd like a word.

Bev kneels beside her

Something's wrong.

Bev What's the matter?

Grace I didn't see Gilbert yesterday.

Bev It's a lot to come every day, Grace. He's probably having a break.

Grace No. It's not like him. Not without telling me. And he would have rung —
said something to someone. No — something isn't right and I'm concerned.

Bev Fair enough — no more said than done.

Grace What will you do?

Bev Wave my magic wand, what else?

Marlene Well you're the first bloody fairy I've seen with a black eye.

Bev Then you haven't lived, Marlene. My God you haven't lived.

Bev exits, laughing

Marlene Oh she's a girl, i'n' she?

Pause

Don't worry, Grace. She'll sort it out for you if anybody will.

Grace He's never missed coming before — not once.

Marlene Pity he didn't have anyone to share it with. Like Bev said, see —
it's a lot for the one to keep coming all the time. And I mean he's like you,
i'n' he — Gilbert now, I mean. He's no spring chicken, is he? Mind you
— the way I'm feeling this morning I think I'm past the sell-by date myself.

Grace (*half listening*) We don't eat chicken. Gilbert and I are vegetarian.

Marlene I wish Roy was — I'd save a fortune. It's nothing for me to spend
fifteen pounds on meat — and that's just for the weekend.

Grace (*amazed*) Just for Sunday lunch?

Marlene No no — Saturdays is in that as well. Then there's the cooked meat,
see. And he eats faggots like he's eating grapes. I've told him — it's you
who should be in here, not me, I said. His bowel system is like Trawsffy-
nydd Nuclear Power Plant. *And* it smells like it sometimes.

Grace Flatulence is nothing to be ashamed of.

Marlene Oh he's *not* ashamed of it. He'll tell you himself, he's proud of most
of 'em.

Pause

Lucy's been gone a long time.

Grace (*pathetically*) I wish *I* could have a bath.

Marlene (*encouragingly*) Why don't you ask 'em then? Bev will sort it out
if you ask her tidy.

Grace (*shaking her head*) There's mirrors in there. I have realized they're keeping them from me. I'm sure I must look dreadful.

Marlene You look all right to me.

Grace Do I really?

Marlene If I could get out of this chair on my own, I'd come over and comb your hair for you.

Grace You do realize it's a wig.

Marlene But it's a very good one, Grace.

Grace I lost it all you see — with the treatment. Bit of a mess, is it?

Marlene It'll be all right if it had a comb run through it.

Grace If only *I* could come to you.

Marlene Don't try it. You stay where you are. Bev will comb it nice for you now when she comes back.

Grace Do you have a comb there?

Marlene Yes — I'll throw it to you.

Grace No — better I throw it to *you*.

Grace takes off her wig and tosses it over to Marlene. It lands on Marlene's bed. Poor Grace looks strange now, with only wisps of hair here and there

Marlene (*reaching for the wig and combing it*) It's a lovely one, Grace. Bet you paid a lot of money for this.

Grace They wanted to give me a hospital issue, but when I put it on Gilbert thought I looked like Joan of Arc. I thought I looked more like Rin-tin-tin. Gilbert insisted on my having something decent.

Marlene It's nice — you only get what you pay for see, don't you? I bought a wig once. Remember when they were all the go in the seventies? Roy used to make fun of it. I kept it for years. I gave it away in the end.

Grace Charities are usually grateful for anything like that.

Marlene I gave it to a boy across the road to make a Guy. Come to think of it *that* looked a bit like Joan of Arc as well.

Grace And I presume it suffered the same fate.

Marlene I don't think Joan of Arc was pushed around by a gang of kids in an orange box.

Lucy enters. She has just had a bath. She hangs her towel over the back of her chair

Marlene There you are. I was beginning to wonder if they'd drowned you.

Lucy I'm sure they forgot me. Still, I enjoyed the soak.

Marlene I'll be glad when they'll let *me* have a bath. I can't see it happening for a bit yet, though. Not till I've had my stitches out at least. And there's something to be said for a blanket bath — even if it *is* only the nurses that do it. What do *you* say, Grace?

Grace I won't even undress in front of Gilbert. We've been married fifty-four years and he has never once seen me naked.

Marlene Oh, you're one of these that likes the light out, are you?

Grace I insist on it. Well I used too. There hasn't been any point for such a long time now.

Marlene Do me a favour, Luce and put this back on for Grace?

Lucy turns and is shocked to see Grace without her wig. She reluctantly takes the wig from Marlene and places it on Grace's head

Lucy I've just seen Doctor Fairwater.

Marlene Yes, I heard he was here. I'm waiting for him to come round. I want to ask him about the wedding.

Lucy Oh, I think he's gone.

Pause

Marlene What do you mean?

Lucy He's finished for the day, I'm sure.

Marlene But he haven't set foot in here.

Lucy I heard Sister say, "See you tomorrow, then", as he disappeared through the double doors.

Marlene (*shrugging it off*) Oh he's probably told her it's all right for me to go. A busy man like him — no need to see me to tell me that see, is there?

Lucy (*to Grace*) There you are. All right?

Grace How do I look?

Lucy Very nice.

Grace If only I could see for myself.

Marlene I think I'll try and get up.

Lucy Do you think that's wise?

Marlene If I show 'em I can get about — that's bound to help 'em make up their mind. In case they're not sure what to do.

Lucy I'd stay where you are if I were you. Apart from the operation, your body is still full of the anaesthetic.

Marlene I'll be all right. (*Referring to the drip*) I can always hang on to this thing. (*She grabs hold of it and manages to scramble to her feet*)

Lucy (*crossing to the foot of Marlene's bed*) Oh, be careful.

Grace Stay where you are, you silly woman!

Marlene You got to show 'em what you can do. They'll keep you in here till God knows when otherwise.

Grace You'll do more harm than good.

Marlene (*determined*) I'm not missing that wedding, Grace. Not for all the tea in China, I'm not. (*With great difficulty she manages to walk to the foot of the bed. Pleased with herself*) How's that?

Lucy How do you feel?

Marlene Buggered up.

Lucy Leave it at that. Perhaps you can go a bit further tomorrow.

Marlene (*resting her behind on the end of the bed*) I'll be all right. I'll just have a spell by here a minute.

Lucy Let me help you back to your chair.

Marlene No, I'll be all right ... I'll be all ... (*She is in such pain that she falls forward*)

Lucy (*panicking*) Oh ... (*To Grace*) What should we do now?

Grace Buzz for a nurse.

Lucy crosses to R *of her bed and presses her buzzer*

Silly thing ought to have known better.

Marlene (*still in the same position*) I'm all right — don't panic, I'm all right.

Grace Anyone with any common sense will know *she's* not going home at the weekend.

Lucy (*crossing back to Grace*) Oh don't say that.

Grace Well it's true, and she's only fooling herself to think otherwise.

Lucy You've got to have a goal.

Grace Even in this ward?

Lucy Especially in this ward. It's pointless just sitting back and letting things happen — it's good to have something to aim for.

Grace I've gone through all that. There's no way out in the end.

Lucy Don't talk like that.

Grace It's all right for you now. You wait until it's *your* turn.

Pause

Lucy Don't you have any faith?

Grace I lost it around about the same time I lost my hair.

Lucy There's no need to be cynical.

Grace It makes you like that after a time.

Marlene attempts to move from the bed

Lucy No Marlene — don't move. Wait till someone gets here.

Marlene (*exhausted*) Lucy — you can help me back in my chair, if you want

to. Don't let 'em see me like this. I'm all right — I'm not hurting. But don't
let 'em see me like this.

Lucy helps Marlene back into her chair then sits on her own bed

Oh thank you — thank you. Don't say nothing now, will you? When they
come, keep your mouth shut, right?

Grace They ought to be told. You may have done yourself a serious injury.

Marlene I'll do *you* a serious injury if you say anything. Got me?

Grace I'm only thinking of your own good.

Marlene I know what's good for me. If I can be in that church on Saturday —
(*she pauses to get her breath*) ... Being there is going to do more for me than
a couple of days' rest in this place.

Grace The whole event will be too much for you.

Marlene I think *I'll* be the judge of that.

Grace But you're not. The situation is out of your hands.

Marlene When it comes down to it the final decision is mine.

Lucy (*scornfully*) Marlene! You'd be silly not to listen to the doctors.

Marlene Only one daughter I've got, look.

Lucy I don't think Roy would let you sign yourself out anyway, if that's what
you're thinking.

Marlene *Roy* wouldn't have a say in it, either.

Lucy You're trying too hard. (*To Grace*) Maybe they'll allow her home in
a wheelchair.

Marlene That's right — a wheelchair. That'll do. I don't care how I go as
long as I get there.

Grace Why didn't they postpone?

Marlene They didn't know I was going to be stuck in here, did they? Nobody
knew. Could hardly cancel with a couple of days to go.

Lucy I still don't think it's out of the question.

Grace Well I do.

Marlene (*to Lucy*) Just don't say anything about what's happened.

Lucy I'm not.

Marlene That goes for you too, Grace. You open your gob and you can comb
your own hair in future.

Grace I don't have a future.

Lucy (*to Marlene*) Oh God, she's down today.

Grace (*insisting*) No I'm not. I'm not at all depressed. I'm a fair age. I have
no complaints. I just wish I'd stop this shilly-shallying and go. I can't bear
anything dragging on.

Lucy I don't know what to say to you anymore.

Grace You can tell me the truth.

Lucy I've never lied to you, Grace.

Grace You're lying now. You humour me, that's all you do. You and that one there.

Lucy (*giving up; turning to Marlene*) Let me put a blanket over you. (*She attempts to do so*)

Marlene No — I don't want it. I don't want anything that might make me look worse.

Bev enters

Bev Somebody buzzed?

No-one answers

Somebody buzzed?

Lucy Well er ...

Marlene No.

Grace Yes.

Pause

I was wondering about Gilbert.

Lucy is relieved, but would still like to be out of the situation. Bev crosses to Grace's bed and plumps up her pillow

Lucy I think I'll just pop down to the day room and swap my magazine. Marlene — what about you?

Marlene Yes, I wouldn't mind a read. (*For Bev's benefit*) I'm feeling a lot better today.

Lucy Grace? Would you like something?

Grace waves her hand dismissively

Lucy exits

Grace (*to Bev*) Do you have any news?

Bev Not yet, but Sister have rung the police station.

Grace (*alarmed*) Police station?

Bev They're sending someone round. They'll ask your husband to ring you so as you don't worry.

Grace When?
Bev Straight away, I imagine.
Grace But you haven't heard anything yet?
Bev I'll let you know the minute I do, Grace, OK? (*She makes to leave*)
Marlene Doctor Fairwater have been and gone then?

Bev nods

He didn't show his face in here.
Bev (*moving to Marlene's bed*) No, but he's gone over your notes with Sister.
Marlene I wanted to see him.
Bev He's a very busy man, Marlene.
Marlene What's going to happen now, then?
Bev I'm not with you.
Marlene About me. Have he said if I can go home or what?
Bev Sister is going to have a word with you when she's got a minute.

Pause

Marlene She's going to tell me I can't go, isn't she? (*She pauses*) I feel
    marvellous, honest I do.
Bev (*sitting on the side of the bed and holding Marlene's hand*) Sister did
    mention about Saturday to Doctor ... but he wouldn't hear of it, love. He
    wouldn't take the responsibility of discharging you.
Marlene Then I'll take it myself.
Bev Look ... I know you're disappointed.
Marlene Two hours — that's all I want to go out for.
Bev Have a word with Sister when she comes.
Marlene (*trying not to be upset*) What's the point? She's only going to come
    and say the same thing.
Bev Better to stay and get well, Marlene.
Marlene (*crying now, but silently*) But I wanted to be there.
Bev Of course you did.
Marlene (*still crying*) She needs me see, Bev. All daughters need their
    mother on their wedding day.
Bev I'm sure she'd rather have you better so she can need you another time.

Pause

Well am I right?

Bev hands Marlene a tissue. Marlene nods, blows and dries her nose

Lucy enters with two magazines. She puts one down at the foot of Marlene's bed as she passes it

Marlene I suppose I knew all along they wouldn't let me go.
Bev (*standing up*) Another week and you might have swung it.

Pause

Marlene You can tell Sister she haven't got to bother to come and see me. She's a busy woman and I don't like her very much anyway. I'm glad it come from *you* though.
Lucy Yes. You've got a way about you.
Bev Oh go on.
Lucy (*insisting*) No, you have. (*To Grace*) Haven't she Grace?
Grace I beg your pardon?
Lucy I said Bev have got a way about her.

Grace doesn't answer

I bet you love your job, don't you?
Bev You've got to. You'd never be able to stick it otherwise.
Lucy Everybody likes you.
Bev Now you're embarrassing me.
Lucy No they do. You've only got to listen to 'em talk in the day room. No-one has a bad word to say about you. Mind you, it wouldn't pay them to or they'll have Marlene to reckon with.

Bev makes a face as she moves to go

Marlene No don't go. Have five minutes with me?

Bev stays. Pause

Hey listen ... what are you working on Saturday?
Bev I'm not, I've got it off.
Marlene (*disappointedly*) Oh, I thought you'd be here when our Louise comes.
Bev I will if you want me too.
Marlene Will you? You can see her dress then ... and you might get a look at her brother if he comes with her.

Bev That settles it. Wouldn't miss it for the world.

Marlene (*with new enthusiasm*) Well, if I can't go to the wedding, I can't go.

Lucy (*sitting on her bed*) That's the spirit.

Marlene But I'm still going to have my hair done though.

Bev That'll be nice.

Lucy Perhaps we all will.

Grace Even me.

Marlene Can we, Bev, what do you think?

Bev I don't see why not.

Marlene We will then. I can still make a bit of a fuss even if I am stuck in here.

Lucy Of course you can.

Grace I'm quite looking forward to it.

Marlene Will you ask Sister if we can have clean covers? That'll make it look a bit better, won't it, and I'll make sure we've all got some nice fresh flowers. Oh I hope to God the weather'll stay nice for her.

Lucy Oh and me.

Marlene We'll have a couple of photos done too, so you make sure you're here now, Bev — I want you to be in them as well. (*She gets really excited*) Oooh, I'll dress up to the nines.

Bev You can put your new outfit on.

Marlene Oh you should see it Bev, it cost a fortune, mind — I look a million dollars in it.

Bev I bet.

Grace And she paid over forty pounds for her hat.

Marlene I did yes, so I think I'd better wear that as well, don't you? What you think girls? Go the whole hog, i'n' it? (*Shouting*) Yeah.

The Lights begin to fade slowly as everybody shouts, joining in with Marlene

Music: "Emergency Ward 10"

Black-out

ACT II

SCENE 1

The same

The following Saturday afternoon, about 3.20 p.m.

As the House Lights fade we hear the last few bars of "Stand By Your Man"

Radio voice-over And that was for Marlene Morgan, whose daughter
Louise got married earlier today ...

There is a sudden and loud burst of church bells as the Lights come up

*All three women are lying on their beds, sleeping and snoring. Grace and
Lucy are both wearing their dressing-gowns, while Marlene is wearing her
wedding outfit, complete with gloves and her forty pound hat. She is not
attached to the drip any longer. Louise's bouquet is on the bedside cabinet—she
and her new husband visited Marlene earlier and left some time ago.
Marlene now has a portable television by her bed*

*After a moment, a Domestic enters wheeling a tea-trolley. Throughout the
following, the Domestic takes tea to Marlene, then Lucy, then Grace. Once
that is finished, she takes bread and butter to them in the same order. When
that task is completed, she strikes water jugs from each bedside. She is about
to place a cup and saucer on Marlene's locker when Marlene wakes*

Marlene Oh ... tea, is it?
Domestic Bread and butter?
Marlene Oh God no, nothing to eat. Listen to these two.

Lucy and Grace continue to snore

I'm lucky to sleep a wink. What time is it?
Domestic Twenty past three.
Marlene Is it indeed. I've been laying for nearly an hour trying to drop off.
Were you here earlier on?

Domestic I've been here all day. Just coming to the end of my shift now though.

Marlene Saw my daughter then, did you?

Domestic (*nodding*) Oh, she looked beautiful.

Marlene She paid a thousand pounds for that dress. I told her when she bought it, "It's lovely", I said. "It's beautiful, but you're off your head paying that kind of money". (*Amazed*) A thousand pounds. "Think what you could have done for your house with that", I said. She haven't got a washing machine. "I'll bring my dirty washing over to you," she said. (*She laughs*) I don't mind — I've got an automatic so it's only a question of shoving it in. I've told her, "You can do your own ironing though," I said. I don't mind helping out but you've got to draw the line somewhere see, haven't you? (*She pauses*) You thought she looked nice then?

Domestic All brides are lovely, aren't they?

Marlene I wasn't. Oh I thought I was done up like a dog's dinner at the time — but when I think of it now ... You should have seen me. I got married in a loose fitting salmon-pink crimplene two-piece suit. Kids today don't know they're born, do they? I mean, for a thousand pounds she could have furnished her house from top to bottom. But they won't have second-hand these days. If it's not new they don't want to know. She had the chance to buy a beautiful fridge for forty pounds. No. I'd rather go without, she said. You should have seen it — there wasn't a mark on it — a real cop. I said to Roy, I said, if ours wasn't working so well I'd have bought it myself, I said. (*She pauses*) Listen to me chopsin' by here. If I don't let you get on every bugger else's tea will be cold.

The Domestic makes to go

Er ... where have you come from now? What I mean is ... have you been to ward six or are you on your way there?

Domestic No, I've been.

Marlene How's her husband doing? (*She nods in Grace's direction*)

Domestic Who is he?

Marlene Bed fourteen. Gilbert 'arris. Or *H*arris as she likes to say. He fell in the house a couple of days ago.

Domestic I know — broken femur, but he's fine I think.

Marlene I'll tell her now when she wakes up. She'll be glad to hear that. See you tomorrow then, is it?

Domestic God willing.

She exits

Marlene takes a sip of tea. Lucy and Grace continue to snore

Marlene I can't stick this much longer. (*Calling to Lucy*) Oi! Rap up, will you?

Lucy (*gently opening her eyes*) Oh ... did I drop off?

Marlene Drop off? You were snoring so much I thought you were in a coma.

Lucy I don't snore.

Marlene (*looking at Grace*) She don't think *she* does either.

Lucy I'm glad you woke me, though. I wasn't having a very nice dream. I dreamed I was going home — but when I got there my house wasn't there. No matter how hard I tried I couldn't find it. People I knew didn't recognize who I was ... it was awful.

Marlene Oh, there you are then. There's a cup of tea by there. Drink it. You'll feel better after that.

Lucy (*sitting up to drink her tea*) I wonder what it means. They say all dreams have meanings.

Marlene Do they? I dreamed I was playing the piano like hell last night and I can't read a word of music.

Lucy Perhaps you've always wanted to. Deep down.

Marlene Do you think so?

Lucy nods

Oh I don't know.

Marlene takes the bouquet from the locker and admires it

Lucy It really is lovely, isn't it?

Marlene Have a guess how much.

Lucy I wouldn't have a clue.

Marlene Forty-seven pounds fifty.

Lucy Good God.

Marlene Lot of money i'n' it? She could have bought a second-hand fridge for that. Mind you, she'd have looked bloody funny walking down the aisle with a fridge on her arm. (*She laughs*)

Pause

Lucy She's a beautiful girl.

Marlene Well, you know, *I* like to think so.

Lucy She isn't like you at all, is she?

Marlene is gobsmacked for a second

What I mean is, I hadn't noticed until this morning how like your husband she is.

Marlene Now you're not the first to notice that. When she was younger she was his spittin' image.

Pause

Didn't notice anything else this morning, did you?

Lucy Like what?

Marlene With Roy. (*She pauses*) I thought he was a bit quiet.

Lucy It was probably nerves. I mean he's never given away a daughter before.

Marlene No it wasn't that. (*She pauses*) He was staring at me. And every time I caught his eye he looked away. Not straight away, like — he wasn't that obvious, but it must have happened at least half a dozen times. And then when he came back here after the reception ... (*she breaks off*) He didn't seem himself at all. Something's wrong.

Lucy He seemed all right to me.

Marlene He hadn't had a drink. Just the toast. That's all he said. He haven't touched a drop of beer.

Lucy That's what it was then — he was sober.

They both have a laugh, but it is clear Marlene is concerned

Pause

Marlene It wasn't just this morning, mind. I've noticed it before. He's been a bit strange for a day or two, now.

Lucy Well, you know him better than anybody.

Marlene Louise was all right, and Darren seemed OK — it's just Roy that didn't seem right.

Lucy I'm sure it's nothing to worry about.

Marlene You do though, don't you? You've got all the time in the world to worry in this place.

Lucy You're probably over-reacting.

Marlene And now he've said he's not going to the do tonight. They got a disco and a running buffet for two hundred and fifty people. Couldn't ask them all to the wedding, see, so they've had them to the fling in the night. Roy was looking forward to it — now he's not going.

Lucy He probably feels it wouldn't be the same without you.

Marlene And the strangest thing of all is, he said he's coming back here. "No need for that", I said. Well I think you heard me, didn't you? "You go and enjoy yourself", I said. I'm not funny like that, see. But no — he've insisted. Back here he's coming and back here he's going to stay, he said.

Lucy I think he's missing you.

Marlene (*suspiciously*) Well it all seems bloody funny to me. I mean Roy's not that type. To miss me, like. Or if he is he'd never show it — not for a minute. He's *never* been able to show feelings like that. He does have 'em. He just can't express 'em, that's all.

Lucy Which is why he's coming back here tonight and not going on to the celebrations.

Marlene Maybe. (*She pauses*) Do you know something? He's never once told me he loves me? Not once. Not once in twenty-five years. Oh he've been jealous, mind. Stopped me doing the gypsy tango with Jackie Turner from the Non Pol once — so I suppose he shows he cares in *that* way. It's just that it would be nice if he actually came out and said it. God, I'd be grateful if he wrote it down. (*She pauses*) Do you know what he wrote on my anniversary card last year? It was our twenty-fifth. "To Marlene, Happy anniversary — all the best — Roy". Didn't even have a bloody kiss on the bottom. Didn't even have a card till our Louise went out and got him one. (*Slight pause*) He's always been the same though — never made a fuss. See all these by here? (*She points to all the "get well" cards displayed on the headboard of the bed*) Not one is from him. It's not that he's tight or doesn't want to send me one. (*Mimicking him*) "What do you want a card from me for? I'd feel so bloody soft, mun". (*She tries to laugh*) I can hear him now.

Lucy There's a lot of men like that. I blame it on their mothers.

Marlene How's that?

Lucy It's the way they're brought up ... School is to blame, too. We're taught early on to play roles, aren't we? Boys have to be tough and play cowboys and Indians and girls, shop and house.

Marlene Not me, love. I'd rather play cowboys any day. A regular Annie Oakley — that's me ... You're right though, I s'pose. Perhaps it does all 'ark back to school days.

Pause

He doesn't even say he loves me when we're ... you know.

Lucy looks vague

(*Persisting*) You know ... I'm glad then though, mind. It would be easy to say it at a time like that. I'd rather hear it out of the blue. It would mean a lot more then ... He nearly told me once. Years ago now, before our Louise was born. We were on a bus of all things. It was Palm Sunday and we were coming back from the cemetery ... I lost a little boy, see. Christopher. He was only four months. Spit of Roy ... None of us said anything for a long time. I was staring out of the window and I don't know where Roy was looking, but our minds were together. We turned and looked at each other at the same time. Uncanny it was. I knew he wanted to say he loved me then — I could see it in his eyes. It was in his mouth — on the tip of his tongue. (*She pauses*) We stared at each other for a long time. Is he going to say it, I thought? Yes he is — no he's not, yes he is — no he's not — (*very excited*) yes he is! Then the bus screeched, swerved, ran over a sheep and *that* put pay to *that*.

Grace stops snoring and wakes up

Grace What time is it?

Marlene Awake at last, are you?

Grace I feel quite horrid.

Marlene There's a cup of tea by there for you. Gone cold now though no doubt.

Grace (*sitting up*) Did someone say the time?

Lucy It's twenty-five to four.

Grace Is it still Saturday?

Marlene Good God, you haven't been sleeping that long. (*She goes to Grace*) Ooohh, hey — I was talking to the domestic when she brought the tea and I asked her about Gilbert. She said he's doing all right but he's broken his femur.

Lucy Oh that *is* a shame.

Marlene I think it's marvellous — it could have been his neck.

Grace I told him to leave the damn decorating alone.

Marlene It's always the same, i'n' it? Just when you're doing all right life comes and kicks you in the shin.

Grace He had a thing about me coming home to a freshly decorated bedroom — and now look where it's led to.

Lucy He only wanted to make everything comfortable for you.

Grace (*suddenly*) What about Boris?

Marlene Who's Boris? (*She sits on the edge of the bed*)

Grace He can't be left in the house by himself.

Lucy (*to Marlene*) She always said she didn't have any family.

Marlene (*to Grace*) He lives with you then, does he, this Boris?

Grace Did Gilbert mention anything? Perhaps he's made arrangements. Oh dear ...

Marlene Listen, Gilbert was by himself in the house when they found him. (*To Lucy*) Ring for Sister. Somebody had better ring this Boris and explain, like. He'll be wondering what the hell has happened to Gilbert. Is he your side of the family or his?

Grace Boris is our cockatiel.

Marlene Your cock what?

Lucy It's a bird.

Marlene (*to Grace, laughing*) Is that what you're on about? A bloody bird?

Grace He might have enough food and drink for a few days — but with a broken femur, Gilbert is going to be in here for months.

Marlene pulls out a bed stool from under Grace's bed and sits on it

Lucy Would he have left a key with anyone? A neighbour looks after my cat.

Grace We've had him for seventeen years.

Marlene Look, don't worry about it. I'll go up and see Gilbert after. Ten to one he've done something about him.

Lucy They're a bit like cats in a funny sort of way, aren't they? Birds.

Marlene and Grace look at each other, then at Lucy

I mean they're not like dogs at all.

Pause

Marlene No, Luce — I'll say that — a dog is nothing like a cat or a bird.

Lucy Dogs are so much more dependent.

Grace I hope he's still in his cage. Gilbert likes to let him out as often as he can. It's just possible he was flying around when Gilbert had his fall. If that's the case, heaven knows what might have happened to him.

Lucy They're a worry, aren't they? Pets.

Marlene They're good company though. Dog I got. Nothing posh, like — Heinz fifty-seven that's all he is, but I can't move for him. Under my feet all day. Even follows me to the toilet.

Lucy (*to Grace*) Does the bird talk?

Grace Can't utter a syllable — but he sings his heart out.

Lucy You think it would say something after seventeen years.

Grace It's the hens do all the talking.

Marlene Just like us then in other words. (*She laughs*) No bugger can get a word in edgeways once *I* start.

Grace Yes, that's true.

Marlene I've always been the same. Never short of something to say, me.

Grace But sometimes it's nice not to hear anything. (*She pauses*) So much can be said with just a look.

Marlene Now I know exactly what you mean by there.

Grace You get quite a lot of that in this place — and not only from the staff. Your own family get to do it in the end. (*She pauses*) Nothing of any seriousness is ever discussed. It's all hidden away in touch or a smile. Everything is said in the gaps and the glances.

Marlene I hope you're not getting morbid again, are you?

Grace Nobody understands, but there comes a time when certain things *have* to be talked about. Arrangements will eventually have to be made, but no-one is prepared to speak about it. You notice that. (*She pulls herself together*) Everything has to be in apple pie order or you just don't rest.

Marlene I'm sure Gilbert have got everything sorted out.

Grace I hope so. If he hasn't he's not going to be able to do anything about it now.

Lucy Don't you have any other family at all?

Grace We have a godson. William. But he's in Detroit, that's in America. We keep in touch. We usually write to each other about once a month. He knows I'm in here but he has no idea why. He thinks I'm having digestive problems, which isn't exactly a lie.

Lucy Wouldn't you like to see him again?

Grace Oh of course — but it's such a long way to come. We had a letter from him last week. Gilbert brought it in but I haven't felt up to reading it yet. (*She gestures towards the cabinet where it is*) He's such a dear boy — works terribly hard.

Marlene Doing well for himself, is he?

Grace He's very successful. Runs a company that manufactures mobile homes. Caravans to you.

Marlene You're pretty close then, even though he lives so far away.

Grace He's the nearest thing I'll ever have to a son.

Marlene Well I think you're cruel.

Grace Pardon, dear?

Marlene If he's as close to you as you say you are to him, I think it's awful he haven't been told how bad you've been.

Grace What's the point of worrying him?

Marlene What's going to happen now with Gilbert stuck in here as well?

Grace It's his femur he's broken not his wrist.

Pause

Marlene I suppose he gets everything, does he, when something happens to you and Gilbert?

Lucy Marlene! You shouldn't be asking things like that.

Marlene I'm only asking to make a point. (*To Grace*) Well am I right? Does he get the lot?

Grace Everything, yes. Lock stock and barrel.

Marlene Well I'd be mortified if I found out that someone I cared for had been awful bad and they never showed me. You might have got your reasons for not wanting him to come and see you, but have you thought about him and his feelings? No — mortified I'd be if anything was to happen and all I thought was wrong with you was you couldn't swallow. If he knew the score I bet he'd be over here like a shot.

Grace (*quietly*) Oh I'm sure he would — but Gilbert and I have decided not to tell him and that's an end to the matter.

Pause

Marlene You're afraid, aren't you? For him to see you.

Pause

Grace I looked so healthy when he saw me last.

Marlene Do you think he'd care for a minute what you looked like?

Pause

Grace *I* care.

Marlene But you look all right. Doesn't she, Luce?

Lucy You're looking a lot better today.

Grace You don't understand, do you? If he were to walk in here this minute, as much as I'd like him to — and he were to see me ... I'd see my reflection in his face ... and I would die.

A pause

Marlene slowly moves back to her bed and sits on it, L

Suddenly Bev rushes on, dressed in off-duty clothes. She hides a small package behind her back

Bev Here you are, Marlene — a prezzy for you. (*She reveals it*)

Marlene For me? What you got?

Bev Open it and find out.

Marlene Oh I love presents, I do.

Bev hands the package over and Marlene opens it

  Photos? (*Very excited*) Not of Louise? How did you have 'em so quick?
Bev I took them into town. Only takes an hour.
Lucy Oh can I have a look as well?

Marlene, Bev and Lucy sit on the end of Marlene's bed. Grace gets up and starts to make her way over

Marlene (*excited*) Oh look at me by there.
Bev There's a better one than that.
Marlene Nice one of you, Luce. (*She hands it to her*)
Bev (*to Marlene*) That's it — look at you in that one.
Marlene (*screaming with laughter*) I look bloody awful. You caught me
   looking funny by there *and* the flash made my eyes red. It's a nice one of
   Louise, though. And *you've* come out nice, Bev. You take a lovely photo
   you do. Oh and there's one of us all together, look. Don't Louise look
   something in that dress? Worth every penny in the long run, see. Oh God —
   (*she screams*) look at Roy in this one. (*She laughs*)

*All four are in very high spirits as they pass the photos around. Plenty of ad-
libbing, etc. Grace is confused by one of the photographs and points it out to
Marlene*

Grace Who is that?
Marlene (*looking at it*) Well that's me, that is. And Bev, look. We're all in
   that. Who took that one I wonder?
Bev Roy, I think.
Marlene (*still looking at the same photograph*) And there's Lucy standing
   next to Darren — and Bev by there see, looking quite jealous.
Bev (*laughing*) Go on.
Marlene Yes you are. Say the truth — you couldn't take your eyes off him.
Grace But who is this here? (*She points*)

*Marlene looks at the photo then at Bev. Bev turns her head to see who it is.
There is a very awkward moment as they both realize Grace is asking about
herself*

Slow fade to Black-out. Music: "St Elsewhere"

SCENE 2

The following Thursday, 9.00 p.m.

When the Lights come up, Marlene is nowhere to be seen. Lucy and Grace are both in bed. Marlene's portable television is on and the music for the BBC's nine o'clock news is heard

Lucy (*to Grace*) Shall I turn it off?

Grace doesn't reply

I think I will. (*She gets up and turns off the television, then hovers about*) I can't it watch these days — it's always so depressing. I can remember when they always used to slip in some light-hearted things. Now it's one mugging after the other — when they're not showing you starving children and burnt out cars on the M4. (*She shrugs*) Oh, perish the thought ... Raymond will be using that motorway tomorrow. Still — he's a very careful driver. (*She goes over to Grace*) Are you all right, Grace?

There is no answer

(*Taking hold of Grace's hand and touching her forehead*) Grace?

Still no answer

Would you like anything?
Grace (*quietly*) I wish I could go to sleep and never wake up.
Lucy (*gently scorning her*) Grace ... no, don't say that.
Grace I'm tired and I've had enough.
Lucy You mustn't give in. You're a fighter — don't let it get the better of you now.
Grace Everything has gone wrong. It was all right before Gilbert was ill.
Lucy Gilbert is doing all right — (*she sits on the bed stool*) There's no need to worry about him.
Grace They don't tell you everything. They said it's only a broken femur but heaven knows what else it might be.
Lucy That *is* all that's wrong with him, Grace, honestly. Marlene has seen him, remember. If there was anything else to worry about *she'd* know what it was. Don't you think?

Grace She wouldn't tell me if there *was* anything.

Lucy Maybe not, but she'd tell me and she hasn't said a word. There really isn't anything to be bothered about. Even that nice little ambulance man is taking care of Boris.

Grace Do you think that's true? They say so many lies here in hospital.

Lucy I'm sure they don't.

Grace Oh nothing malicious. I know they do it to protect you.

Lucy It's Gilbert who told Marlene about Boris, remember. You don't think *he'd* lie to you, do you?

Pause

Grace No — perhaps not.

Pause; Lucy makes to move away

(*Sighing weakly*) Oh dear ...

Lucy (*turning back to her*) What is it?

Grace I feel so ill.

Lucy Are you in pain?

Grace I'm sure I'm due for another injection. I'll try and hang on until then. She's been gone a long time. Where has she gone?

Lucy (*sitting down again*) Who knows. Probably making tea for the entire wing.

Grace Well her heart's in the right place.

Lucy Yes.

Grace Shame about her mouth.

Lucy (*smiling*) Grace!

Grace She talks too much. She's not a bad old thing but she talks too much.

Lucy She keeps us going anyway, doesn't she?

Grace It would be a duller place here without her, I'm sure. Why am I so hot?

Lucy Shall I buzz and ask for a fan?

Grace I feel really ... odd.

Pause

Something strange happened earlier on. I'd dozed off — but then I woke up. I could hear you talking, but I couldn't open my eyes. I was wide awake and aware of everything but my eyelids remained closed. I couldn't even move my limbs.

Lucy Maybe you were only dreaming you were awake. I've heard it happens sometimes.

Grace (*insisting*) No I *was* awake, I tell you. I can even repeat what you were talking about. She — (*she means Marlene*) was pumping you for information about your son. And you were telling her how he owns your house. How he bought it for you several years after your husband passed on. I heard it all but I could do nothing but lay here ... I relaxed, thinking ... well if this is some kind of coma perhaps I'm on my way, so to speak. I couldn't tell myself to close my eyes because they were already shut. I thought I may just as well give in and not fight it when I must have dropped off to sleep again. When I eventually woke up everything was back to normal. Isn't that strange?

Lucy moves back to her own bed

You *were* telling her about your son and your house, weren't you?
Lucy Yes — yes I was.
Grace And it's happened before. That is about the fourth time this week.

Marlene enters, pushing in a portable telephone (on a trolley)

Marlene (*revealing it as if she was a magician's assistant*) Darra!! (*To Lucy*) Look what I found. All I got to do is plug it in for you and you're away.
Lucy *I'm* away?
Marlene Well I brought it for you.
Lucy I don't want to make a phone call.
Marlene You haven't *said* you want to make one, but I can read between the lines. I'm a mother myself. I know you're dying to talk to him really.
Lucy To who?
Marlene To Raymond. Don't try and tell me it's not eating you away.
Lucy What's not?
Marlene Tomorrow. His visit. Why he's coming down. Go on — tell me it's not bothering you.
Lucy Of course it's bothering me — but I can wait until tomorrow.

Pause

Marlene Well no harm in ringing.
Lucy I don't know the number.
Marlene Directory enquiries. You can have a little chat to him anyway. (*She plugs the phone in*)
Lucy No.
Marlene Perhaps *he's* got something to tell *you*.
Lucy Whatever he has to say, he'll say it tomorrow.

Marlene Well it's up to you of course ... but don't you think it'll be better to know what it's all about *now*? What do they say — forearmed is forewarned?

Pause

Lucy I've been thinking about it. Whatever his reasons for coming down I'm sure it's nothing to worry about.

Pause; Marlene ponders what to do next

Marlene (*moving round in front of the phone*) Look, it's no good — I've got to tell you.

Lucy looks at her

I'm quick see, Lucy. I've always been sharp like that.
Lucy What are you talking about?
Marlene I don't know how to tell you this ... I've had an idea there was something up for a bit now. *And* of course you do tell me little bits now and then like ——
Lucy What are you trying to say?

Pause

Marlene I know where you live, right? I already knew the street but I didn't know the number till you said it the other day. I asked our Roy to go past it on his way down here, like, you know — when he was coming to visit me?

Pause

It *is* number sixty-two, i'n' it?

Lucy nods, not knowing what to expect

Elizabeth Street?

Lucy nods again

That's right then.

Pause

Well he's got it up for sale, love.

Lucy sits on her bed

Lanyons Davies and Evans are handling it. Thirty-seven and a half thousand. Roy phoned 'em this morning. You're leaving all your carpets and curtains, but you're taking the light fitting in the front room.

There is a terrible pause

Lucy I'm leaving most of the furniture too.
Marlene What?
Lucy Well I won't be needing it, will I?

Pause

Marlene You mean you know about it?
Lucy I've been asking him to sell it for months. He wouldn't put it on the market until he'd finished the alterations to his house. He's making his study bigger and turning it into a bedroom for me.

Pause

Marlene Oh, there you are then.
Lucy I wouldn't be at all surprised when he comes tomorrow if I don't end up going back with him.
Marlene So you did know about it then?
Lucy What?
Marlene The sale of the house.
Lucy Yes. But it's not *my* house remember.
Marlene No. (*She pauses*) Still don't want to ring him?

Lucy makes a face as she smiles and nods her head

(*Incredulously*) Oh well, there you are then. (*She pushes the phone trolley to the foot of her bed. Pause. She crosses to Grace*) How are you, Grace? All right?
Grace No, I'm dreadful.

Marlene What's the matter? Anything I can do?

Grace I'd like a paper hanky.

Marlene (*looking through the locker*) You've run out. Don't worry though —
I got plenty.

Grace No. There is another box inside.

Marlene (*finding a new box of Kleenex, then a letter*) Oh ... look at this. (*She
takes the letter out and shows it to Grace*) You've got a letter by here.

Grace It's from William.

Marlene I guessed it was, 'cos of the airmail. (*She opens the box of tissues
and hands one to Grace*) Here you are. (*She pauses*) Shall I read it to you?

Grace Would you?

Marlene Yes, love. I don't mind at all as long as I can understand his
handwriting. Just let me get my glasses. (*She gets them, then sits on the bed
stool next to Grace's bed, then opens the letter. Reading with an American
accent*) "Hi there!" (*She, laughs then resumes in her own accent*) "Got
your letter last week and was glad to hear that everything is OK now with
you, Grace, and that you're out of hospital at last." (*She looks up at Grace*)

Grace Go on, go on.

Marlene "I was only saying to Mim" — who's Mim?

Grace His wife.

Marlene Funny name.

Grace Just get on with it.

Marlene (*reading*) "I was only saying to Mim just a few days ago how
worried I was getting. But I guess I can ease up a little now that you're home
and doing just fine. Things have been really hectic here — sales have gone
through the roof, so needless to say it's a very busy time for me right now.
Things should ease up in a couple of months and only then will normality
be restored."

Lucy dozes off

"Mim and I plan a vacation then so you can be sure we'll come over and
visit. Six years is a long time and we're anxious to see you both. We went
to Jaynie's graduation since I wrote you last. She looked beautiful — I
know if you'd seen her you'd have been proud. We took a couple of shots
and I've enclosed one." There's a photo.

She places it in Grace's hand but Grace doesn't look at it

"Maybe we'll bring her over with us when we come. Mim and I thought
we'd hire a car and take you both up to the Lake District for a week, maybe.
Wouldn't that be just great?"

Grace's head falls sharply to the left

"Well it's something for the two of you to think about. Maybe you can let me know your thoughts when you next write. Anyhow, I'm going to sign off now. Mim has cooked a meal and the whole house is full of its wonderful smell. Lots of love and kisses, William, Mim and Jaynie." Ahhh. (*She looks up*) I wonder what she cooked.

Silence

Grace?

There is no reply. Marlene calls her again, louder this time. Lucy wakes and moves to L of Grace's bed

Grace — can you hear me?

Lucy What's wrong?

Marlene I thought she was upset 'cos of the letter — but she doesn't look right to me.

Lucy Press the buzzer.

Marlene You saw her. She was all right just now, wasn't she? (*She presses the buzzer*) Mind you, saying that, she've been going down hill a bit lately.

Lucy Ever since they brought Gilbert in.

Marlene Well thereabouts. (*She tosses Grace's letter on to her own bed*)

Lucy It is only the femur with Gilbert, isn't it?

Marlene As far as I know. Why?

Lucy She was worried about it. Said to me earlier on that she was afraid it was something more.

Marlene No — it's just the femur. Anything else I'd have found out by now.

Lucy That's what I said. It's a shame they can't get together and see each other. But I don't suppose it's possible to get her up to *his* ward.

Marlene I don't know — but they'd never be able to bring him here. Not in the state he's in. In a couple of weeks perhaps ...

Lucy I think that might be too late then, don't you?

Marlene They're stopping the treatment now, did she tell you?

Lucy Why are they doing that?

Marlene The body can only take so much, see, Lucy. It doesn't sound very good, does it?

Lucy Careful! Don't let her hear you.

Marlene I don't think she can hear anything.

Lucy No — she might be having one of her turns. She was telling me about them just now.

Marlene She looks completely gone to me.
Lucy You mean she's ——
Marlene No, she's still breathing. She's just out for the count, that's all.

Bev enters

Bev What's the problem, girls?
Marlene (*grabbing her*) Come and have a look at Grace.

Bev quickly examines Grace then takes her pulse

She was all right one minute, and the next ——
Bev How long have she been like this?
Marlene Oh I don't know ... about five minutes? It is about five minutes, Luce, i'n' it?

Lucy nods

Yes, about five minutes. I buzzed you straight away — I didn't hang about.

Marlene leans right over Grace and lifts her eyelid

Bev Don't do that, Marlene.
Marlene You want to check her eyes. Have a look and see if they've dilated.
Bev Why don't you go to your bed, Marlene.

Pause

Marlene Are you being funny to me?
Bev Course I'm not. I don't like the look of this.
Marlene I was saying to Lucy — well we were both saying — she haven't been looking right for a couple of days. (*She lifts Grace's wrist and checks her pulse*)
Bev I'm going to have to insist you go back to your bed, Marlene. (*She takes Marlene by her elbow and moves her towards her bed*) I want to have a proper look at Grace and I don't want you under my feet. (*She goes back to Grace's bed and draws the curtains around it so that neither she nor Grace can be seen*)
Marlene She *is* short with me — I don't care what she says. I can tell in a minute, I can.
Lucy She's only doing her job.

Marlene Well I wasn't going to stop her. Helping her — that's all I was doing. (*She lies down*)

Lucy They don't like anyone interfering.

Marlene (*outraged*) Bloody good job I *did* interfere. God knows how long she'd be left laying like that if I hadn't noticed and buzzed to tell 'em.

Lucy There's no need to be offended.

Marlene *I'm* not offended. But it would be nice to be appreciated now and again. This sort of thing goes on all the time, you know.

Lucy What sort of thing?

Marlene Patients keeping an eye on each other. Some of these nurses wouldn't know what was going on half the time if it wasn't for people like me. Oh I'm not saying I want 'em to thank me every two minutes — but like I said see, Lucy, it wouldn't do 'em any harm to realize how much they depend on patients like us.

Pause

Do you know something?

Lucy What?

Marlene I *am* offended.

Lucy She only asked you to go back to your bed.

Marlene Yes but me and her are butties. I could take it off any other nurse.

Lucy Well it's about time someone put you in your place.

Pause

Marlene What do you mean?

Lucy I know you're trying to be good, but you go too far sometimes.

Marlene (*amazed*) I do?

Lucy People don't always need it.

Marlene What?

Lucy That little push you always want to give them. I know you mean well but ——

Marlene If you've got something on your chest I think you'd better come out and say it.

Lucy I don't want to quarrel with you ——

Marlene I know what it is. (*She gets up and crosses to Lucy*) You didn't like it because I brought you the phone. That's it isn't it?

Lucy I didn't mind you bringing the telephone at all. I *did* mind though, you asking Roy to have a look at my house. It's none of your business. It's got nothing to do with you but you still had to go and poke your nose in!

Pause

Marlene (*quietly*) You didn't know he put the house up, did you?

Pause

Lucy No. But I'm sure I'm right. I will be going to live with him when I leave here.

Bev appears from behind the curtains and starts to leave

Marlene (*leaping back on to her bed*) Everything all right, "Nurse"? I don't want to interfere — I'm only concerned, that's all.
Bev I'm going to get Sister. I'm concerned about her as well.

She exits

Lucy (*confidentially*) Do you think she's taken a turn for the worst?
Marlene *I'm* afraid to open my mouth gone.

Pause

Lucy Peer in. See what she looks like.
Marlene You do it. I might get accused of something.
Lucy I hope we're not going to fall out.
Marlene I thought I was doing you a favour.
Lucy I'm sure you did.
Marlene I'll learn my lesson though.
Lucy Do you think so?

Pause

Marlene (*laughing a little*) I can't help myself. That's me — that's how I am and there's nothing I can do about it.
Lucy You'll get in hot water one day.
Marlene Oh I hope so — I haven't had a bath since I've been here.

They both laugh

Lucy I hope nothing is going to happen to her.

Bev returns with Sister. They speak to no-one and walk briskly to Grace's bed. Marlene gets up and goes towards Grace but Sister quickly shuts the curtains to prevent her from looking in

Marlene (*turning back to Lucy*) It would have to be her!
Lucy Oh, she's all right.
Marlene It must be me then, 'cos Bev won't have nothing said about her either.
Lucy Bev won't have anything said about anyone.
Marlene True. She's good like that, i'n' she. I've asked her to come and visit me and Roy when I get out of here. I don't know whether she will, mind.
Lucy Did she say she would?
Marlene She didn't say she wouldn't.
Lucy Well she probably will then.
Marlene "You don't live that far from us", I said. It's only twenty minutes over the mountain in the car. She got a Fiat Panda.
Lucy What's that?
Marlene You've seen the trolley that comes round with our food?

Lucy nods

Well it's a bit like that with doors. Big enough for her though, no doubt. It's only her and her fella see, i'n' it? (*She moves to Lucy's bed, pulls over a chair and sits in it*) She was telling me the other night, when we were having a cup of tea together in the solarium, that things have come to a head.
Lucy With who?
Marlene Her and that boy she's with. I opened a packet of McVitie's half-covered and she told me everything. Spilt the lot, she did. She's been having a hell of a life with him, I s'pose. And the best part about it, it's her house. Chuck him out, I said. I wouldn't put up with it. (*She pauses*) He's still there though from what I can gather. She haven't done anything about it yet as far as I know.
Lucy She probably still thinks a lot of him. It's hard to let go if you still feel like that. When you love someone it's easy to let them get away with murder.
Marlene Well it's never easy but I know what you mean. It doesn't matter what they do behind your back — he's still your son and you'll always love him. Well am I right or am I right?

Pause

Lucy I wonder how Grace is.

Marlene I can't see Gilbert lasting long if anything happens to her, can you?

Lucy No, they are devoted, aren't they?

Marlene I wonder why they never had kids.

Lucy She told me that she was one of nature's little treasures.

Marlene What did she mean by that?

Lucy I don't know, and I didn't like to ask.

Pause

Marlene She should have someone with her ... you know, family like, at a time like this.

Lucy Having children is no guarantee that they'll be there for you when you need them.

Marlene Well I'd like to think that *my* two would be around.

Lucy All mothers hope that. The truth is that it doesn't always happen.

Marlene Well let me put it this way ... God help our Darren and Louise if they're not there for *me* when I need 'em.

Lucy You stand a better chance than some. The odds go up a lot if you've got a girl.

Pause

Marlene If I was seriously ill like Grace, I'd want somebody close to be with me, wouldn't you?

Lucy Oh yes. It's not a time for being on your own.

Marlene Right, well that settles it then. (*She gets up, tucks the chair under Lucy's bed, gets the phone, takes it* c, *plugs it in and then dials the international operator*)

Lucy What are you doing?

Marlene Get a pen and paper, will you? I want you to write this down.

Lucy (*getting a pad and pencil from her handbag*) What are you up to now?

Marlene Pass my purse out of my locker too. This is going to take a couple of fifty pences.

Lucy (*getting Marlene's purse and handing it to her*) Tell me what you're doing.

Marlene I'm running some hot water, right? And if I scald myself I scald myself.

Lucy stands next to Marlene, pencil and paper at the ready

(*Into the phone*) Hallo. Operator? Yes. Get me the code for Detroit!

Black-out. Music: "The Young Doctors"

SCENE 3

The following Saturday, around eleven a.m.

When the Lights come up, the curtains are around Grace's bed. Almost immediately they are opened (by Bev), to reveal June lying on the bed, wearing a dressing-gown, and Bev, who, having asked some preliminary questions, is writing on the record sheet. She has a fairly large white envelope tucked under one arm. Marlene is not in the ward. She is about to be discharged, and her weekend case is on her bed, packed. Lucy is sitting in an armchair near her bed. She looks trance-like, staring into mid air

Bev *(to June)* ... Oh and religion — I've forgotten to ask you that.
June I don't believe.
Bev *(writing)* OK — atheist. Right, well you're down for an X-ray. I have sent for a porter so it shouldn't be too long. Anything you want to ask me?

June shakes her head

You know my name. I'm Bev. You remember me from last time, don't you?
June Yes.
Bev If you need anything, just buzz. *(She replaces the records on the foot of the bed. To Lucy)* No idea where Marlene went, Lucy?
Lucy She might have said where she was going, but I didn't take much notice.
Bev *(crossing to Lucy)* Oh what's the matter, love? You don't seem your usual self this morning.
Lucy Oh I'm all right — you don't have to worry about *me*.
Bev *(remembering)* Of course ... I know what it is. You're disappointed because you weren't able to go home with your son yesterday.

Pause

Oh never mind — it was nice to see him anyway, wasn't it? And between me and you I don't think you'll be too long in here now. Maybe a week at the most.

Pause

I see she's got her case out. Is she all packed and ready to go?

Lucy She's been ready for about two hours.
Bev I expect you'll miss her too, won't you? We all will.

Marlene enters. She is wearing a shell-suit and a pair of trainers. She seems a little out of sorts

Talk of the devil ...
Marlene I thought I just saw Roy going into the Sister's office.
Bev (*crossing to Marlene*) Yes ... Doctor Fairwater wants to explain your medication.
Marlene So he's come to fetch me, has he?
Bev Nice little surprise, isn't it?
Marlene When was all this arranged then —? 'Cos the last thing I said to Roy was to book a taxi to fetch me at quarter past eleven. There was no mention of him taking a day off work yesterday.
Bev Sister had a quick word after visiting last night.

They share a look. Marlene knows there's more to all this. Bev doesn't offer any more information

Bev (*handing her the envelope*) Look. I got this for you. It's from Roy.
Marlene From Roy? What is it? ... Is never a card?
Bev Open it.
Marlene (*opening it; moving to her bed*) What's he sending me a card for? (*She reads it, obviously touched*) "Welcome Home". (*She opens it to read what's inside, then looks up at Lucy and Bev*)
Lucy (*sitting on her bed*) What does it say?
Marlene (*fighting back a tear*) "To Marlene. Welcome home, all the best ... Roy." (*She blows her nose*) Guess what ... I got a kiss this time. Only one, but it's a start. (*She pulls herself together and smiles as she reads the front of the card again*) "Welcome Home". (*Trying to make light of it*) That's a laugh. I bet I can't get in the kitchen for dirty dishes.
Bev It's like a palace there — he told me.

Marlene sighs and unzips her case to put the card inside. Bev starts to strip Marlene's bed

Marlene I've been to see Grace.
Lucy How is she?
Marlene Not very good. That's what they told me, anyway — they wouldn't let me in ... I went to say so long to Gilbert too. I wasn't going to mention nothing about Grace but he already knew all about it 'cos of the godson.

Lucy Fancy coming all the way from America.

Marlene Nice of him to come in here and thank me, wasn't it? (*To Lucy*) Handsome boy, i'n' he? What he sees in that Mim though, I *don't* know. Still—one man's meat, I s'pose ... (*To Bev*) Do you think he meant it when he asked me to come and visit him in America?

Bev I don't think so.

Marlene Why not?

Bev Well it wasn't a real invitation.

Marlene (*insulted*) What do you mean?

Bev As I remember it, Marlene, you more or less invited yourself.

Marlene No way I did.

Bev I was here, Marlene. I heard it all.

Marlene Did he or didn't he say that me and Roy can come over and stay with him any time?

Bev What *he* said ... or rather what *you* said went something like this—"Oh ... Detroit. I've heard such a lot about it. Do you know—and this might sound a bit of a coincidence—but I've always wanted to go to America? Funny i'n' it? And I was only saying to Roy the other day, I said. 'The air fare isn't a problem', I said. But you've really got to have someone out there to go to, haven't you? Family like, you know. Or a friend. Or even a friend of a friend. Someone who'd be kind enough to meet you off the plane, put a roof over your head and show you the sights". And to that he said—well, if ever you find yourself over there, give him a call and maybe you can all meet up. Now that's hardly an invitation to stay with him in Detroit.

Marlene (*crossing her legs*) Well it's good enough for me. Anyway, it wouldn't be for a year or two.

They look straight into each other's eyes

Apart from all the expense I've just had with the wedding, I've got to get out of the woods first.

Pause; the stare continues

I need a little break though, so I thought I might book your caravan for a week. How does that grab you?

Bev (*smiling*) I don't normally let it out.

Marlene Now you know I'd look after it.

Bev It's nothing grand.

Marlene Well that's all right 'cos I wouldn't want anything posh—not with Roy and the dog.

Pause

Well, are you going to let me have it or not?

Bev You are a human bulldozer, you know that, don't you?

Marlene I take it that means yes then, does it? We can talk about the details when you come and see me next week.

Bev Oh, I'm coming next week am I?

Marlene Well you'll have to if you want your deposit for the van. Don't just turn up though. Let me know when you're coming so's I can make sure Darren is around.

Bev You're naughty, you are.

Marlene Go on, I know you like him, and he can't take his eyes off you when he's here.

Bev I've got to get on.

Marlene I haven't given you my address.

Bev I'll be back. You'll see me before you go, don't worry. You don't need to give me your address anyway — I'll get it from records.

She exits, taking the dirty sheets with her

Marlene (*sighing*) Hell of a girl, see. (*She takes down all the "get well" cards which are displayed around her bed*)

Lucy She told me *I'll* only be about a week.

Marlene (*pleased to hear it*) Oh, there you are.

Lucy At least that's time enough for Raymond to make his arrangements.

Marlene (*going to her*) Listen, love — there's nothing wrong with sheltered accommodation. Roy's mother was in it for years. Loved it, she did. Five pounds for a television licence and a warden at your beck and call, you won't know you're born.

Pause

Oh I know it's not what you had in mind — but, well, *I* wouldn't *want* to leave the valleys, anyway. Between me and you you can shove Surrey up your arse. Wouldn't give you tuppence for it. Take it from me, you'll be better off down here.

Pause

S'cuse me a minute. (*She goes to June, still with the cards in her hand*) I hope you won't be offended or anything.

June looks up from a magazine

But I was wondering if you'd like to have these. (*She holds up the cards*) Only I noticed when you were in here last that you didn't have any ... To be honest with you they're not all mine. Three or four of 'em was still on the bed when I came in. (*She puts some of them on the headboard of June's bed*) Shall I put 'em up by here for you? I won't say nothing if you won't. Let 'em think you're popular, i'n' it? (*She displays more cards*) Still having problems then, are you?

June Pardon?

Marlene I had a shock to see you back in so soon ... Same trouble I s'pose?

June doesn't answer

Remember Grace? She was in this bed up till last Thursday. They got her in a little room on her own now. She took a turn for the worst. It's only a matter of time. Come in by ambulance, did you?

June (*firmly*) Yes.

Marlene What was the matter with Robert then? It is Robert, i'n' it? I remembered his name right — Robert? Not convenient, I take it.

June I wonder would you do something for me?

Marlene Yes love — anything — what do you want?

June (*shouting*) Will you just fuck off!

Marlene is gobsmacked. She looks over at Lucy and then back at June

Marlene Want me to leave you alone, do you?

June doesn't answer

(*Crossing to Lucy's bed*) She's a bit upset. Thought she'd seen the last of this place see, I s'pect.

Pause

Lucy They're going back home today. Raymond and Hazel.

Marlene Oh ... what time are they coming.

Lucy doesn't answer

They are calling in before they go?

Lucy They said they would, but I don't think they will.
Marlene Why not?
Lucy They know in their hearts what they're doing is wrong.

Pause

He needs the money, he said ... He'll lay low for a bit now. If I know him, he'll ring the hospital and leave a message saying that he's had to go home straight.
Marlene Kids — I don't know. Do they never stop breaking your heart?
Lucy I always thought Hazel was behind it all. I used to think she was behind everything he did — but she's not. He's doing what he's doing and he is what he is without any help from her ... it's all his doing, and that twists the knife that little bit more.
Marlene Well try and look at it this way, Luce — you don't live with 'em, you've got bugger all to thank 'em for.

Pause

I reckon he'll be here, anyway. I can't see him phoning without saying so long.

Bev enters with a wheelchair

Bev June? You ready, love?

June gets up from the bed and sits in the wheelchair

Right then, let's get you off to X-ray. (*To Lucy*) Ooh, Lucy, there's been a phone call for you. Your son wants you to give him a ring. Sister's office is still busy or you could use the phone in there. I'm sure I saw the portable down in the day room though. OK June ... fasten your seatbelts — it's going to be a bumpy ride. (*She winks at Marlene*)

She exits, wheeling June

Pause; Marlene and Lucy look at each other

Marlene (*crossing to Lucy*) Well ... you going to ring him?
Lucy It's only to tell me he's not calling in.
Marlene What if it's not? Perhaps he's ringing to say he's not going to sell the house after all. He could have had second thoughts.

Lucy (*shaking her head*) If that was the case he wouldn't have left a message. He'd have been here in person.

Marlene So you're not going to ring him then?

Lucy Oh, I probably will. I'd rather I didn't but I probably will.

Marlene Got ten pences?

Lucy There's plenty in my purse.

Marlene Going to go now, are you?

Lucy Just as well. (*She reaches for her purse on her locker*)

Marlene I expect I'll be gone by the time you come back.

Lucy Yes ... well take care of yourself.

Marlene And you.

Pause; they hug each other. They are both genuinely touched

Don't take any bloody nonsense off him now mind. If you're right and he's not coming to see you before he goes — tell him straight. Only one mother he's got and you might not always be here ... None of us are here for ever, love.

They share a look

Lucy exits. As she goes she passes Bev coming in

Bev All done?

Marlene The doctor finished with Roy?

Bev Not quite.

An awkward pause

Marlene Is he all right? Roy?

Bev I've just come from there and he's fine. (*She touches Marlene's arm*) He's very positive about it and I think *you* should be too.

Marlene Oh I am. If anybody's going to beat this thing it's *me*.

Bev (*smiling*) I bet you are.

Another awkward pause

Marlene When are they going to start treatment?

Bev That's what he's telling Roy now. I think in about a fortnight.

Marlene (*trying to make light of it*) I wonder should I buy one my own colour or should I go for a change. (*She touches her hair*)

Bev You're going to be all right.

Marlene I know I am ... What about you?

Pause

Bev I took your advice. There was one almighty row, but I told him to be gone
  by the time I come home from work today.
Marlene Good for you. You're too nice to be treated like that. You won't
  be sorry.
Bev (*making a face — not knowing if she agrees*) I don't like coming home
  to an empty house.
Marlene Nor our Darren.

They look at each other and laugh

Bev You don't give up, do you?
Marlene It wouldn't pay me to, love ... Well ... I'm ready. (*She gets her
  suitcase from her bed*)
Bev Give me that.
Marlene There's nothing in it, hardly.
Bev I'll take the telly then.
Marlene No, I'm not having it now. I told Lucy she can have a lend of it while
  she's still in. You can put it by there for her if you like.

Bev picks it up and puts it by Lucy's bed

  She said she'd give me a ring when to fetch it.

Pause

Bev Right then — come on — I'll walk out with you.
Marlene Er, no ... I'm not being funny or anything but I'd rather go on my
  own. I walked in by myself and I want to walk out the same way ... Silly,
  i'n' it?
Bev Not at all.

Pause

  I'll see you then.
Marlene When?
Bev Soon.
Marlene When?

Bev Friday.
Marlene You won't forget?
Bev You won't let me. (*She turns to leave*)
Marlene (*remembering; just as Bev reaches the door*) Er ... Darren does
   weights on a Friday.
Bev Thursday?
Marlene Great.
Bev Half-past seven.
Marlene I'll have the kettle on.

They stare at each other as Bev smiles and nods

   Bev exits

*Marlene is alone in the ward and the place seems strangely quiet. After a
short moment, she takes her case, has one last quick look around and walks
out, quite determinedly. As soon as she is out the door she starts talking with
all the energy and verve that is still so much part of her character*

   (*As she goes, then off*) Hallo Emrys, how are you? Back again I see. Having
   another inch cut off are you?

We hear her laughter off as Shirley Bassey sings "This is My Life"

Black-out

CURTAIN

FURNITURE AND PROPERTY LIST

ACT I
SCENE 1

On stage: Beds with linen, pillows, curtains, etc. *Under them:* bed stools
Lockers. *In them and on them:* "get well" cards, water jugs, tissues, flowers, fruit, plastic rubbish bags, make-up bags, personal belongings, buzzers, etc.
Chairs
Colour television (**June/Bev**)
Weekend case. *In it:* clothes, personal belongings, etc. (**June**)
Bottle of squash (**June**)
Fruit (**June**)
Carrier bag (**June**)
Sponge bag. *In it:* toiletries, etc., bag of cotton wool balls

Off stage: Bed (**Bev** and **Nurses**)
Magazine (**Marlene**)
Lucy's locker (**Bev**)

ACT I
SCENE 2

Strike: Fruit

Set: Surgical paper hat (**Marlene**)
Letter (**Lucy**)
Photograph of Lucy's family
Make-up bag. *In it:* lipstick, rouge, comb, compact (without mirror), etc. (**Grace**)
Handbag (**Lucy**)
Make-up bag. *In it:* compact (with mirror) (**Marlene**)

Personal: **Grace**: wig

ACT I
SCENE 3

Set: Drip (**Marlene**)
Magazine (**Grace**)

| *Off stage:* | Towel (**Lucy**) |
| | Two magazines (**Lucy**) |

| *Personal:* | **Bev**: watch |

ACT II
SCENE 1

| *Set:* | **Marlene**'s portable television |
| | **Louise**'s bouquet |

| *Off stage:* | Tea trolley. *On it:* tea pots and tea cups, bread and butter, etc. (**Domestic**) |
| | Small package containing photos (**Bev**) |

ACT II
SCENE 2

| *Set:* | **Grace**'s letter (**Marlene**) |

| *Off stage:* | Portable telephone (**Marlene**) |

ACT II
SCENE 3

| *Set:* | Weekend case (**Marlene**) |

| *Off stage:* | Wheelchair (**Bev**) |

| *Personal:* | **Bev**: record sheet, envelope containing **Marlene**'s card |

LIGHTING PLOT

Interior. Practical fittings required: none

ACT I, Scene 1

To open: Full stage lighting

Cue 1   **Marlene** looks out front, a worried expression on
             her face   (Page 10)
             Black-out

ACT I, Scene 2

To open: Full stage lighting; late morning effect

Cue 2   **Bev**: " ... when you are Mr DeMille."   (Page 18)
             Black-out

ACT I, Scene 3

To open: Full stage lighting; late morning effect

Cue 3   Everybody begins shouting with **Marlene**   (Page 28)
             Start fade; Black-out when music ("Emergency Ward
                10") starts

ACT II, Scene 1

To open: Fade House Lights with music, then darkness (during radio voice-over)

Cue 4   A sudden and loud burst of church bells   (Page 29)
             Bring up full stage lighting; mid afternoon effect

Cue 5   **Grace**: "But who is this here?"   (Page 38)
             Slow fade to Black-out